# THE ETERNAL SOUL

A compilation of writings by
Bahá'u'lláh, Abdu'l-Baha
and The Báb.

Illustrated by Corinne Randall

intellect

This compilation on the theme of life after death is selected from the writings of Bahá'u'lláh, the founder of the Bahá'i Faith, 'Abdu'l-Bahá his son, and The Báb, his forerunner.

The soul's journey is described as eternal, starting with development in this life and then progressing through all the "worlds of God" until finally it returns to a state of blissful unification with its creator. The cycle is completed but the soul retains its individuality.

These writings highlight the essential role that the prophets and messengers of God have in assisting the soul's progression. The true nature of the next life is beyond anything we can comprehend on this physical plane but the ineffable mysteries alluded to in these quotes, from spiritual exaltation to tears of separation, provide an endless fountain of inspiration for the artistic imagination.

The world of matter is an outer expression or facsimile of the inner kingdom of the spirit. Scientists wonder why the power of gravity is so weak compared to the other forces and explain this by pointing to an unseen force within another dimension working against gravity. 'Abdu'l-Bahá compares gravity, that draws man to the centre of the earth, to the density of the love of self. "The only power that is capable of delivering man from this captivity is the power of the breaths of the Holy Spirit."

The soul is of one indivisible substance and therefore everlasting. Nonetheless, the progress of the soul can only be within its own condition (the condition of servitude). The Baha'i concept envisions salvation as motion itself, the profound joy of being in motion toward godliness. A truly heavenly condition involves an endless progression of fulfilment and enlightenment rather than an end goal of comfort and ease. Heaven is experienced as nearness to God and Hell as distance both in this life and the next.

These writings provide consolation in suffering and bereavement. Abdu'l-Bahá invites us to look forward to death as we may anticipate the goal of a journey and Bahá'u'lláh describes death as a "messenger of joy".

*"Consider death itself the essence of life."*

To consider that after the death of the body the spirit perishes is like imagining that a bird in a cage will be destroyed if the cage is broken, though the bird has nothing to fear from the destruction of the cage. Our body is like the cage, and the spirit is like the bird. We see that without the cage this bird flies in the world of sleep; therefore if the cage becomes broken, the bird will continue and exist. Its feelings will be even more powerful, its perceptions greater, and its happiness increased...

'Abdu'l-Bahá

To consider that after the death of the body the spirit perishes is like imagining that a bird in a cage will be destroyed if the cage is broken, though the bird has nothing to fear from the destruction of the cage. Our body is like the cage, and the spirit is like the bird. We see that without the cage this bird flies in the world of sleep; therefore, if the cage becomes broken, the bird will continue to exist. Its feelings will be even more powerful, its perceptions greater, and its happiness increased. In truth, from hell it reaches a paradise of delights because for the thankful birds there is no paradise greater than freedom from the cage.

*'Abdu'l-Bahá*

O SON OF SPRIT!
Burst thy cage asunder, and even as the phoenix
of love soar into the firmament of holiness.
Renounce thyself and, filled with the spirit of
mercy, abide in the realm of celestial sanctity.


O OFFSPRING OF DUST!
Be not content with the ease of a passing day,
and deprive not thyself of everlasting rest. Barter
not the garden of eternal delight for the
dust-heap of a mortal world. Up from thy prison
ascend unto the glorious meads above, and from
thy mortal cage wing thy flight unto the
paradise of the Placeless.

*Bahá'u'lláh*

Ye are even as the bird which soareth, with the full force of its mighty wings and with complete and joyous confidence, through the immensity of the heavens, until, impelled to satisfy its hunger, it turneth longingly to the water and clay of the earth below it, and, having been entrapped in the mesh of its desire, findeth itself impotent to resume its flight to the realms whence it came. Powerless to shake off the burden weighing on its sullied wings, that bird, hitherto an inmate of the heavens, is now forced to seek a dwelling-place upon the dust.

*Bahá'u'lláh*

O MY FRIENDS!

Have ye forgotten that true and radiant morn, when in those hallowed and blessed surroundings ye were all gathered in My presence beneath the shade of the tree of life, which is planted in the all-glorious paradise? Awe-struck ye listened as I gave utterance to these three most holy words: O friends! Prefer not your own will to Mine, never desire that which I have not desired for you, and approach Me not with lifeless hearts, defiled with worldly desires and cravings. Would ye but sanctify your souls, ye would at this present hour recall that place and those surroundings, and the truth of My utterance should be made evident unto all of you.

*Bahá'u'lláh*

Just as the earth attracts everything to the centre of gravity, and every object thrown upward into space will come down, so also material ideas and worldly thoughts attract man to the centre of self. No sooner does he attempt to soar upward than the density of the love of self, like the power of gravity, draws him to the centre of the earth. The only power that is capable of delivering man from this captivity is the power of the breaths of the Holy Spirit.

*'Abdu'l-Bahá*

The Prophets and Messengers of God have been sent down for the sole purpose of guiding mankind to the straight Path of Truth. The purpose underlying their revelation hath been to educate all men, that they may, at the hour of death, ascend, in the utmost purity and sanctity and with absolute detachment, to the throne of the Most High.

*Bahá'u'lláh*

Waft, unto me, O my God and my Beloved, from the right hand of Thy mercy and Thy loving-kindness, the holy breaths of thy favours, that they may draw me away from myself and from the world unto the courts of Thy nearness and Thy presence.

*Bahá'u'lláh*

In our solar system, the centre of illumination is the sun itself... This central luminary is the one source of the existence and development of all phenomenal things...Without this quickening impulse there would be no growth of tree or vegetation, neither would the existence of animal or human being be possible; in fact no forms of created life would be manifest upon the earth...

Likewise in the spiritual realm of intelligence and idealism there must be a centre of illumination, and that centre is the everlasting, ever-shining Sun, the Word of God. Just as the phenomenal sun shines upon the material world producing life and growth, likewise the spiritual or prophetic Sun confers illumination upon the human world of thought and intelligence, and unless it rose upon the horizon of human existence the kingdom of man would become dark and extinguished.

*'Abdu'l-Bahá*

In the Rose Garden of changeless splendour
a Flower hath begun to bloom, compared
to which every other flower is but a thorn,
and before the brightness of Whose glory the
very essence of beauty must pale and wither.
Arise, therefore, and, with the whole enthusiasm
of your hearts, with all the eagerness of your
souls, the full fervour of your will, and the
concentrated efforts of your entire being,
strive to attain the paradise of His presence,
and endeavour to inhale the fragrance of the
incorruptible Flower, to breathe the sweet
savours of holiness, and to obtain a portion of
this perfume of celestial glory. Whoso followeth
this counsel will break his chains asunder,
will taste the abandonment of enraptured love,
will attain unto his heart's desire, and will
surrender his soul into the hands of his Beloved.
Bursting through his cage, he will, even as the
bird of the spirit, wing his flight to his holy
and everlasting nest.

*Bahá'u'lláh*

Lo, the Nightingale of Paradise singeth upon the twigs of the Tree of Eternity, with holy and sweet melodies, proclaiming to the sincere ones the glad tidings of the nearness of God, calling the believers in the Divine Unity to the court of the Presence of the Generous One, informing the severed ones of the message which hath been revealed by God, the King, the Glorious, the Peerless, guiding the lovers to the seat of sanctity and to this resplendent Beauty.

*Bahá'u'lláh*

I am the Sun of Wisdom and the Ocean of
Knowledge. I cheer the faint and revive the dead.
I am the guiding light that illumineth the way.
I am the royal Falcon on the arm of the
Almighty. I unfold the drooping wings of
every broken bird and start it on its flight.

*Bahá'u'lláh*

O God! O God! This is a broken-winged bird and his flight is very slow—assist him so that he may fly toward the apex of prosperity and salvation, wing his way with the utmost joy and happiness throughout the illimitable space, raise his melody in Thy Supreme Name in all the regions, exhilarate the ears with this call, and brighten the eyes by beholding the signs of guidance.

*'Abdu'l-Bahá*

Those souls that, in this day, enter the divine kingdom and attain everlasting life, although materially dwelling on earth, yet in reality soar in the realm of heaven. Their bodies may linger on earth but their spirits travel in the immensity of space. For as thoughts widen and become illumined, they aquire the power of flight and transport man to the Kingdom of God.

*'Abdu'l-Bahá*

O SON OF MY HANDMAID!

Didst thou behold immortal sovereignty, thou wouldst strive to pass from this fleeting world. But to conceal the one from thee and to reveal the other is a mystery which none but the pure in heart can comprehend.

*Bahá'u'lláh*

Men should hold in their souls the vision of celestial perfection, and there prepare a dwelling-place for the inexhaustible bounty of the divine spirit.

*'Abdu'l-Bahá*

O SON OF MAN!

The light hath shone on thee from the horizon of the sacred Mount and the spirit of enlightenment hath breathed in the Sinai of thy heart. Wherefore, free thyself from the veils of idle fancies and enter into My court, that thou mayest be fit for everlasting life and worthy to meet Me. Thus may death not come upon thee, neither weariness nor trouble.


O SON OF JUSTICE!

Whither can a lover go but to the land of his beloved? And what seeker findeth rest away from his heart's desire? To the true lover reunion is life, and separation is death. His breast is void of patience and his heart hath no peace. A myriad lives he would forsake to hasten to the abode of his beloved.

*Bahá'u'lláh*

By My life, O friend, wert thou to taste of these fruits, from the green garden of these blossoms which grow in the lands of knowledge, beside the orient lights of the Essence in the mirrors of names and attributes—yearning would seize the reins of patience and reserve from out thy hand, and make thy soul to shake with the flashing light, and draw thee from the earthly homeland to the first, heavenly abode in the Center of Realities, and lift thee to a plane wherein thou wouldst soar in the air even as thou walkest upon the earth, and move over the water as thou runnest on the land.

*Bahá'u'lláh*

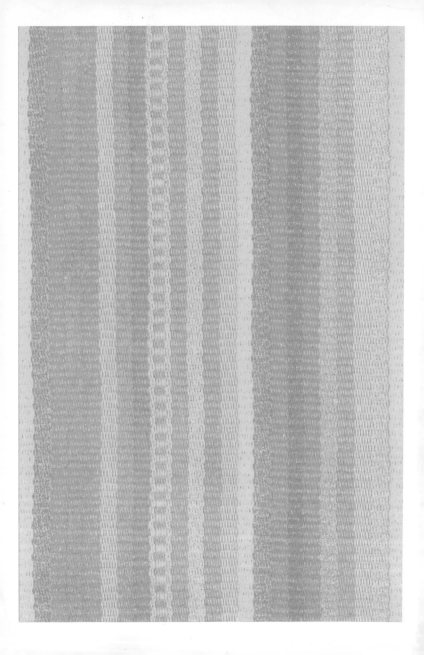

The outer expression used for the Kingdom is heaven; but this is a comparison and similitude, not a reality or fact, for the Kingdom is not a material place; it is sanctified from time and place…The spirit has no place; it is placeless; and for the spirit the earth and the heaven are as one since it makes discoveries in both.

*'Abdu'l-Bahá*

The purpose of God in creating man hath been, and will ever be, to enable him to know his Creator and to attain His Presence. To this most excellent aim, this supreme objective, all the heavenly books and the divinely-revealed and weighty Scriptures unequivocally bear witness. Whoso hath recognized the Day Spring of Divine guidance and entered His holy court hath drawn nigh unto God and attained His Presence, a Presence which is the real Paradise, and of which the loftiest mansions of heaven are but a symbol.

*Bahá'u'lláh*

Whensoever the light of Manifestation of the King of Oneness settleth upon the throne of the heart and soul, His shining becometh visible in every limb and member. At that time the mystery of the famed tradition gleameth out of the darkness: "A servant is drawn unto Me in prayer until I answer him; and when I have answered him, I become the ear wherewith he heareth..." For thus the Master of the house hath appeared within His home, and all the pillars of the dwelling are ashine with His light. And the action and effect of the light are from the Light-Giver; so it is that all move through Him and arise by His will.

*Bahá'u'lláh*

Whoso reciteth, in the privacy of his chamber, the verses revealed by God, the scattering angels of the Almighty shall scatter abroad the fragrance of the words uttered by his mouth, and shall cause the heart of every righteous man to throb. Though he may, at first, remain unaware of its effect, yet the virtue of the grace vouchsafed unto him must needs sooner or later exercise its influence upon his soul.

*Bahá'u'lláh*

O God! Refresh and gladden my spirit. Purify my heart. Illumine my powers. I lay all my affairs in Thy hand. Thou art my Guide and my Refuge. I will no longer be sorrowful and grieved; I will be a happy and joyful being. O God! I will no longer be full of anxiety, nor will I let trouble harass me. I will not dwell on the unpleasant things of life. O God! Thou art more friend to me than I am to myself. I dedicate myself to Thee, O Lord.

*'Abdu'l-Bahá*

...us capt̃ iⁿ carmine eiusdem corone iⁿ qua ē aurea eñt 2 iⁿ ca-

zaphiro sculpta. hn̄s iⁿ gimis duos zapheros 2 duos palacios

corona preśat dn̄s Inuentoꝛ donauit eox ꝑ ornamtõ capitis bō. ext

signa de marx̄ps rege debñt Bociⁿ coronari Item pontiu arare iⁿ e

2 sceptꝛa argnteu̅ deant̄nr 2 anls aureꝰ eⁿ palacio

insignia pontificalia Primo insula cu̅ perl̄ 2 lapidibus ꝑec̃ sta

Reveal Thyself, O Lord, by Thy merciful
utterance and the mystery of Thy Divine Being,
that the holy ecstasy of prayer may fill our souls
- a prayer that shall rise above words and letters
and transcend the murmur of syllables and
sounds - that all things may be merged into
nothingness before the revelation of Thy
splendour.

*'Abdu'l-Bahá*

In the beginning of his human life man was embryonic in the world of the matrix. There he received capacity and endowment for the reality of human existence. The forces and powers necessary for this world were bestowed upon him in that limited condition. In this world he needed eyes; he received them potentially in the other. He needed ears; he obtained them there in readiness and preparation for his new existence. The powers requisite in this world were conferred upon him in the world of the matrix.

Therefore in this world he must prepare himself for the life beyond. That which he needs in the world of the Kingdom must be obtained here.

That divine world is manifestly a world of lights; therefore man has need of illumination here. That is a world of love; the love of God is essential. It is a world of perfection; virtues or perfections must be acquired. That world is vivified by the breaths of the Holy spirit; in this world we must seek them. That is the Kingdom of life everlasting; it must be attained during this vanishing existence.

*'Abdu'l-Bahá*

The rewards of the other world are peace, the spiritual graces, the various spiritual gifts in the Kingdom of God, the gaining of the desires of the heart and the soul, and the meeting of God in the world of eternity. In the same way the punishments of the other world—that is to say, the torments of the other world—consist in being deprived of the special divine blessings and the absolute bounties, and falling into the lowest degrees of existence. He who is deprived of these divine favors, although he continues after death, is considered as dead by the people of truth.

*'Abdu'l-Bahá*

Be generous in prosperity, and thankful in adversity. Be worthy of the trust of thy neighbour, and look upon him with a bright and friendly face. Be a treasure to the poor, an admonisher to the rich, an answerer of the cry of the needy, a preserver of the sanctity of thy pledge. Be fair in thy judgment, and guarded in thy speech. Be unjust to no man, and show all meekness to all men. Be as a lamp unto them that walk in darkness, a joy to the sorrowful, a sea for the thirsty, a haven for the distressed, an upholder and defender of the victim of oppression.

Let integrity and uprightness distinguish all thine acts. Be a home for the stranger, a balm to the suffering, a tower of strength for the fugitive. Be eyes to the blind, and a guiding light unto the feet of the erring. Be an ornament to the countenance of truth, a crown to the brow of fidelity, a pillar of the temple of righteousness, a breath of life to the body of mankind, an ensign of the hosts of justice, a luminary above the horizon of virtue, a dew to the soil of the human heart, an ark on the ocean of knowledge, a sun in the heaven of bounty, a gem on the diadem of wisdom, a shining light in the firmament of thy generation, a fruit upon the tree of humility.

*Bahá'u'lláh*

One day of days We repaired unto Our Green Island. Upon Our arrival, We beheld its streams flowing, and its trees luxuriant, and the sunlight playing in their midst. Turning Our face to the right, We beheld what the pen is powerless to describe; nor can it set forth that which the eye of the Lord of Mankind witnessed in that most sanctified, that most sublime, that blest, and most exalted Spot. Turning, then, to the left We gazed on one of the Beauties of the Most Sublime Paradise, standing on a pillar of light, and calling aloud saying: "O inmates of earth and heaven! Behold ye My beauty, and My radiance, and My revelation, and My effulgence. By God, the True One! I am trustworthiness and the revelation thereof, and the beauty thereof. I will recompense whosoever will cleave unto Me, and recognize My rank and station, and hold fast unto My hem."

*Bahá'u'lláh*

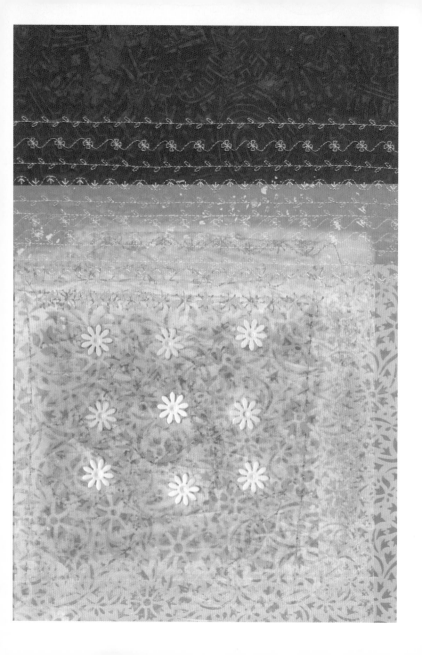

O COMPANION OF MY THRONE!

Hear no evil, and see no evil, abase not thyself, neither sigh nor weep. Speak no evil, that thou mayest not hear it spoken unto thee, and magnify not the faults of others that thine own faults may not appear great; and wish not the abasement of anyone, that thine own abasement be not exposed. Live then the days of thy life, that are less than a fleeting moment, with thy mind stainless, thy heart unsullied, thy thoughts pure, and thy nature sanctified, so that, free and content, thou mayest put away this mortal frame, and repair unto the mystic paradise and abide in the eternal kingdom for evermore.

*Bahá'u'lláh*

did My beauty

... hardew sect, ...

... of all learning

... Readst, and

...

...

... close ...

... is there, and of ...

hallowed beauty of the blessed

... once, that is, to all save thy ...

... das to all save My word; ...

learning are the knowledge of the

... older men, a pure heart and

... that never enter the ...

... Blind the eyes, that thou ...

... beauty; stop thine ears that ...

... into the sweet melody of thy

... of all learning, that the

... of the knowledge, and

... righteous that ...

O SON OF DUST!

Blind thine eyes, that thou mayest behold My
beauty; stop thine ears, that thou mayest hearken
unto the sweet melody of My voice; empty
thyself of all learning, that thou mayest partake
of My knowledge; and sanctify thyself from
riches, that thou mayest obtain a lasting share
from the ocean of My eternal wealth. Blind thine
eyes, that is, to all save My beauty; stop thine
ears to all save My word; empty thyself of all
learning save the knowledge of Me; that with a
clear vision, a pure heart and an attentive ear
thou mayest enter the court of My holiness.


O MAN OF TWO VISIONS!

Close one eye and open the other. Close one to
the world and all that is therein, and open the
other to the hallowed beauty of the Beloved.

*Bahá'u'lláh*

When the true lover and devoted friend
reacheth to the presence of the Beloved,
the sparkling beauty of the Loved One and the
fire of the lover's heart will kindle a blaze and
burn away all veils and wrappings. Yea, all he
hath, from heart to skin, will be set aflame,
so that nothing will remain save the Friend.

*Bahá'u'lláh*

At every moment long ye for non-existence, for when the ray returneth to the sun, it is wiped out, and when the drop cometh to the sea, it vanisheth, and when the true lover findeth his Beloved, he yieldeth up his soul.

'Abdu'l-Bahá

Consider how a being, in the world of the womb, was bereft of any perceptions at all. But once, out of the world of darkness, he passed into this world of light, then his eye saw, his ear heard, his tongue spoke.

In the same way, when the human soul soareth out of this transient heap of dust and riseth into the spiritual world, then veils will fall away, and verities will come to light, and all things unknown will be made clear, and hidden truths be understood.

*'Abdu'l-Bahá*

Know thou of a truth that the soul, after its separation from the body, will continue to progress until it attaineth the presence of God, in a state and condition which neither the revolution of ages and centuries, nor the changes and chances of this world, can alter. It will endure as long as the Kingdom of God, His sovereignty, His dominion and power will endure. It will manifest the signs of God and His attributes, and will reveal His loving kindness and bounty. The movement of My Pen is stilled when it attempteth to befittingly describe the loftiness and glory of so exalted a station. The honour with which the Hand of Mercy will invest the soul is such as no tongue can adequately reveal, nor any other earthly agency describe.

*Bahá'u'lláh*

Such a soul liveth and moveth in accordance
with the Will of its Creator, and entereth the
all-highest Paradise. The Maids of Heaven,
inmates of the loftiest mansions, will circle
around it, and the Prophets of God and His
chosen ones will seek its companionship.
With them that soul will freely converse,
and will recount unto them that which it
hath been made to endure in the path of God,
the Lord of all worlds.

*Bahá'u'lláh*

If any man be told that which hath been
ordained for such a soul in the worlds of God,
the Lord of the throne on high and of earth
below, his whole being will instantly blaze out
in his great longing to attain that most exalted,
that sanctified and resplendent station.

*Bahá'u'lláh*

The light which these souls radiate is responsible for the progress of the world and the advancement of its peoples. They are like unto leaven which leaveneth the world of being, and constitute the animating force through which the arts and wonders of the world are made manifest. Through them the clouds rain their bounty upon men, and the earth bringeth forth its fruits. All things must needs have a cause, a motive power, an animating principle. These souls and symbols of detachment have provided, and will continue to provide, the supreme moving impulse in the world of being.

*Bahá'u'lláh*

It is clear and evident that when the veils that conceal the realities of the manifestations of the Names and Attributes of God, nay of all created things visible or invisible, have been rent asunder, nothing except the Sign of God will remain—a sign which He, Himself, hath placed within these realities. This sign will endure as long as is the wish of the Lord thy God, the Lord of the heavens and of the earth... Just as the conception of faith hath existed from the beginning that hath no beginning, and will endure till the end that hath no end, in like manner will the true believer eternally live and endure. His spirit will everlastingly circle round the Will of God... It is evident that the loftiest mansions in the Realm of Immortality have been ordained as the habitation of them that have truly believed in God and in His signs. Death can never invade that holy seat.

*Bahá'u'lláh*

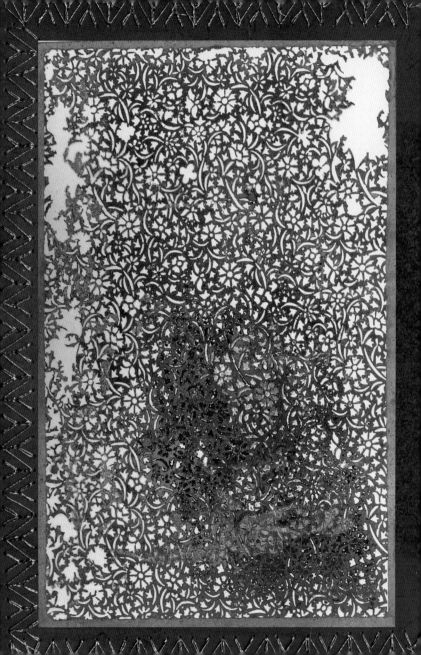

Mortal charm shall fade away, roses give way to thorns, and beauty and youth shall live their day and be no more. But that which eternally endureth is the Beauty of the True One, for its splendor perisheth not and its glory lasteth forever; its charm is all-powerful and its attraction infinite.

*'Abdu'l-Bahá*

The world is like the vapour in a desert, which the thirsty dreameth to be water and striveth after it with all his might, until when he cometh unto it, he findeth it to be mere illusion.

*Bahá'u'lláh*

The worlds of God are countless in their number, and infinite in their range. None can reckon or comprehend them except God, the All-Knowing, the All-Wise. Consider thy state when asleep... thy spirit, having transcended the limitations of sleep and having stripped itself of all earthly attachment, hath, by the act of God, been made to traverse a realm which lieth hidden in the innermost reality of this world. Verily I say, the creation of God embraceth worlds besides this world, and creatures apart from these creatures. In each of these worlds He hath ordained things which none can search except Himself, the All-Searching, the All-Wise.

Now there are many wisdoms to ponder in the dream... First, what is this world, where without eye and ear and hand and tongue a man puts all of these to use? Second, how is it that in the outer world thou seest today the effect of a dream, when thou didst vision it in the world of sleep some ten years past? God, the Exalted, hath placed these signs in men, to the end that philosophers may not deny the mysteries of the life beyond nor belittle that which hath been promised them... Likewise, reflect upon the perfection of man's creation, and that all these planes and states are folded up and hidden away within him.

Dost thou reckon thyself only a puny form
When within thee the universe is folded?

*Bahá'u'lláh*

The Kingdom is the world of vision where all the concealed realities will become disclosed... The mysteries of which man is heedless in this earthly world, those he will discover in the heavenly world, and there will he be informed of the secret of truth; how much more will he recognize or discover persons with whom he hath been associated. Undoubtedly, the holy souls who find a pure eye and are favoured with insight will, in the kingdom of lights, be acquainted with all mysteries, and will manifestly behold the Beauty of God in that world. Likewise will they find all the friends of God, both those of the former and recent times, present in the heavenly assemblage.

*'Abdu'l-Bahá*

The worlds of God are in perfect harmony and correspondence one with another. Each world in this limitless universe is as it were a mirror reflecting the history and nature of all the rest. The physical universe is likewise in perfect correspondence with the spiritual or Divine realm. The world of matter is an outer expression or facsimile of the inner Kingdom of the spirit.

*'Abdu'l-Bahá*

Scientific philosophy has demonstrated that a simple element ("simple" meaning "not composed") is indestructible, eternal...

The soul is not a combination of elements, it is not composed of many atoms, it is of one indivisible substance and therefore eternal. It is entirely out of the order of the physical creation; it is immortal.

*'Abdu'l-Bahá*

The human soul is exalted above all egress and regress. It is still, and yet it soareth; it moveth, and yet it is still. It is, in itself, a testimony that beareth witness to the existence of a world that is contingent, as well as to the reality of a world that hath neither beginning nor end.

*Bahá'u'lláh*

Divine perfection is infinite, the progress of the soul is also infinite. From the very birth of a human the soul progresses, the intellect grows and knowledge increases. When the body dies, the soul lives on.

*'Abdu'l-Bahá*

As to the soul of man after death, it remains in the degree of purity to which it has evolved during life in the physical body, and after it is freed from the body it remains plunged in the ocean of God's Mercy.

From the moment the soul leaves the body and arrives in the Heavenly World, its evolution is spiritual, and that evolution is:
The approaching unto God.

*'Abdu'l-Bahá*

The soul is a sign of God, a heavenly gem whose reality the most learned of men hath failed to grasp, and whose mystery no mind, however acute, can ever hope to unravel. It is the first among all created things to declare the excellence of its Creator, the first to recognize His glory, to cleave to His truth, and to bow down in adoration before Him. If it be faithful to God, it will reflect His light, and will, eventually, return unto Him. If it fail, however, in its allegiance to its Creator, it will become a victim to self and passion, and will, in the end, sink in their depths.

*Bahá'u'lláh*

Know thou that all men have been created in the nature made by God, the Guardian, the Self-Subsisting. Unto each one hath been prescribed a pre-ordained measure, as decreed in God's mighty and guarded Tablets. All that which ye potentially possess can, however, be manifested only as a result of your own volition.

*Bahá'u'lláh*

Every soul will advance and develop until he attaineth the station at which he can manifest all the potential forces with which his inmost true self hath been endowed.

*Bahá'u'lláh*

Man is in the highest degree of materiality, and at the beginning of spirituality—that is to say, he is the end of imperfection and the beginning of perfection. He is at the last degree of darkness, and at the beginning of light; that is why it has been said that the condition of man is the end of the night and the beginning of day... He has the animal side as well as the angelic side, and the aim of an educator is to so train human souls that their angelic aspect may overcome their animal side... Not in any other of the species in the world of existence is there such a difference, contrast, contradiction and opposition as in the species of man.

*'Abdu'l-Bahá*

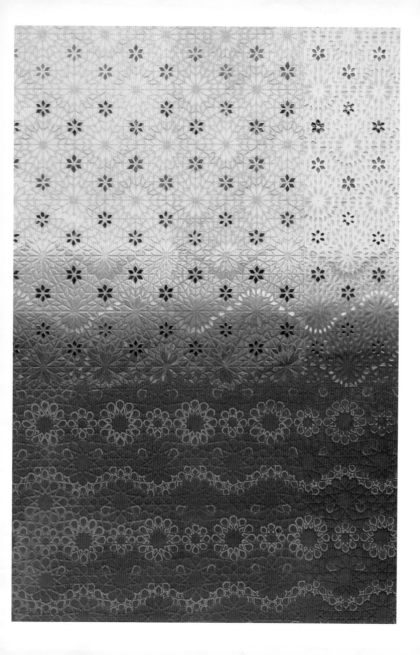

The soul, whether it be in sleep or waking,
is in motion and ever active. Possibly it may,
whilst in a dream, unravel an intricate
problem, incapable of solution in the waking
state.

*'Abdu'l-Bahá*


Each soul is fashioned after the nature of God,
each being pure and holy at its birth...
The spirit of man has a beginning, but it
has no end: it continues eternally.

*'Abdu'l-Bahá*

The difference and distinction between men will naturally become realized after their departure from this mortal world. But this distinction is not in respect to place, but in respect to the soul and conscience. For the Kingdom of God is sanctified from time and place; it is another world and another universe. And know thou for a certainty that in the divine worlds the spiritual beloved ones will recognize each other, and will seek union with each other, but a spiritual union. Likewise a love that one may have entertained for anyone will not be forgotten in the world of the Kingdom, nor wilt thou forget there the life thou hadst in the material world.

*Bahá'u'lláh*

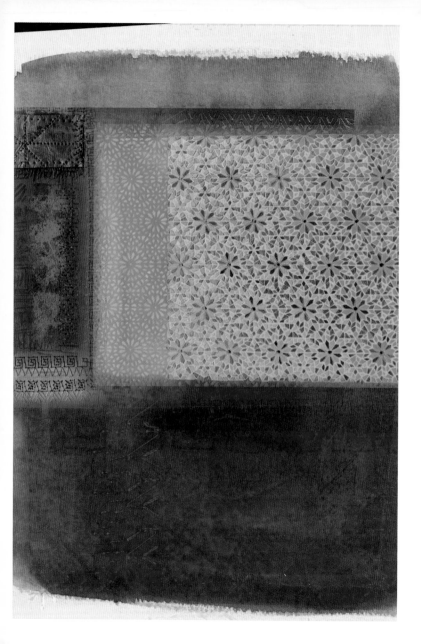

Once the soul hath departed this life, he will behold in that world whatsoever was hidden from him here: but there he will look upon and comprehend all things with his inner eye.

*'Abdu'l-Bahá*

When the soul attaineth the Presence of God, it will assume the form that best befitteth its immortality and is worthy of its celestial habitation.

*Bahá'u'lláh*

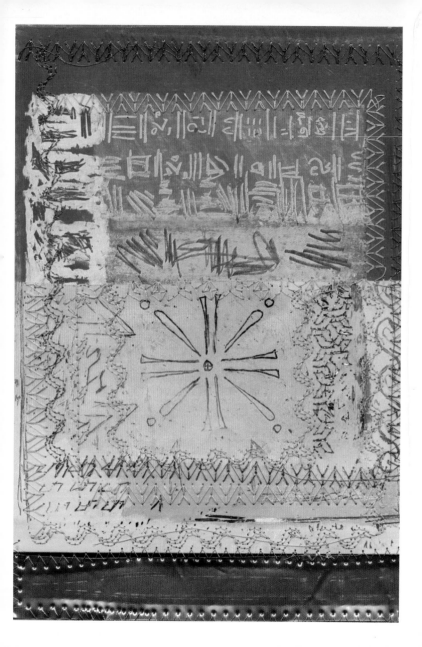

O SON OF BEING!

Thou art My lamp and My light is in thee.
Get thou from it thy radiance and seek none
other than Me. For I have created thee rich
and have bountifully shed My favour upon thee.

O SON OF MAN!

Thou art My dominion and My dominion
perisheth not, wherefore fearest thou thy
perishing? Thou art My light and My light
shall never be extinguished, why dost thou
dread extinction? Thou art My glory and My
glory fadeth not; thou art My robe and My
robe shall never be outworn. Abide then in
thy love for Me, that thou mayest find Me
in the realm of glory.

*Bahá'u'lláh*

A friend asked: How does one look forward to death?

'Abdu'l-Baha answered: How does one look forward to the goal of any journey? With hope and expectation.

At first it is very difficult to welcome death, but after attaining its new condition the soul is grateful, for it has been released from the bondage of the limited to enjoy the liberties of the unlimited. It has been freed from a world of sorrow, grief and trials to live in a world of unending bliss and joy.

*'Abdu'l-Bahá*

O SON OF THE SUPREME!

I have made death a messenger of joy to thee. Wherefore dost thou grieve? I made the light to shed on thee its splendour. Why dost thou veil thyself therefrom?

O SON OF SPIRIT

With the joyful tidings of light I hail thee: rejoice! To the court of holiness I summon thee; abide therein that thou mayest live in peace for evermore.

*Bahá'u'lláh*

As to Paradise: It is a reality and there can be no doubt about it, and now in this world it is realized through love of Me and My good-pleasure. Whosoever attaineth unto it God will aid him in this world below, and after death He will enable him to gain admittance into Paradise whose vastness is as that of heaven and earth. Therein the Maids of glory and holiness will wait upon him in the daytime and in the night season, while the daystar of the unfading beauty of his Lord will at all times shed its radiance upon him, and he will shine so brightly that no one shall bear to gaze at him.

*Bahá'u'lláh*

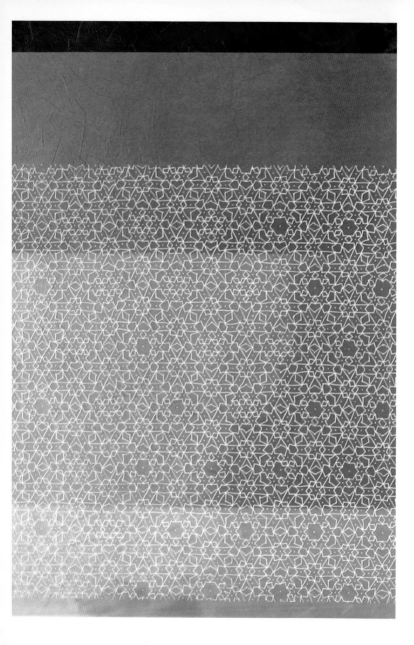

Worship thou God in such wise that if thy worship lead thee to the fire, no alteration in thine adoration would be produced, and so likewise if thy recompense should be paradise. Thus and thus alone should be the worship which befitteth the one True God. Shouldst thou worship Him because of fear, this would be unseemly in the sanctified Court of His presence, and could not be regarded as an act by thee dedicated to the Oneness of His being. Or if thy gaze should be on paradise, and thou shouldst worship Him while cherishing such a hope, thou wouldst make God's creation a partner with Him, notwithstanding the fact that paradise is desired by men.

Fire and paradise both bow down and prostrate themselves before God. That which is worthy of His Essence is to worship Him for His sake, without fear of fire, or hope of paradise.

*The Báb*

There is no paradise, in the estimation of the believers in the Divine Unity, more exalted than to obey God's commandments, and there is no fire in the eyes of those who have known God and his signs, fiercer than to transgress His laws and to oppress another soul, even to the extent of a mustard seed.

*The Bab*

O SON OF BEING!
Bring thyself to account each day ere thou art summoned to a reckoning: for death, unheralded, shall come upon thee and thou shalt be called to give account for thy deeds.

*Bahá'u'lláh*

O SON OF WORLDLINESS!

Pleasant is the realm of being, wert thou to attain thereto; glorious is the domain of eternity, shouldst thou pass beyond the world of mortality; sweet is the holy ecstasy if thou drinkest of the mystic chalice from the hands of the celestial Youth. Shouldst thou attain this station, thou wouldst be freed from destruction and death, from toil and sin.

*Bahá'u'lláh*

The lovers of the Abhá Beauty wish for no other recompense but to reach that station where they may gaze upon Him in the Realm of Glory, and they walk no other path save over desert sands of longing for those exalted heights. They seek that ease and solace which will abide forever, and those bestowals that are sanctified beyond the understanding of the worldly mind.

*'Abdu'l-Bahá*

Those who have passed on through death, have a sphere of their own. It is not removed from ours: their work of the Kingdom, is ours: but it is sanctified from what we call time and place. Time with us is measured by the sun. When there is no more sunrise, and no more sunset, that kind of time does not exist for man. Those who have ascended have different attributes (conditions) from those who are still on earth, yet there is no real separation...

Sincere prayer always has its effect, and it has a great influence in the other world. We are never cut off from those who are there...

In prayer there is a mingling of stations, a mingling of condition. Pray for them as they pray for you.

*'Abdu'l-Bahá*

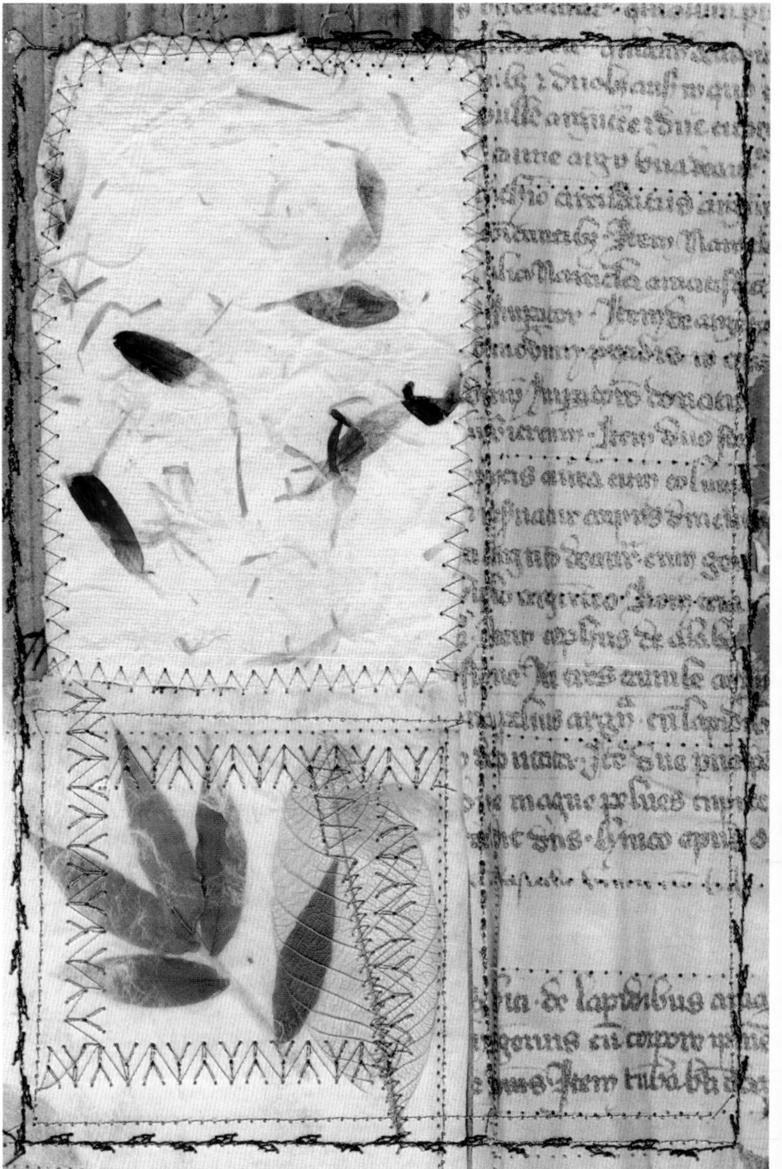

Question.—What is the condition of children who die before attaining the age of discretion or before the appointed time of birth?

Answer.—These infants are under the shadow of the favor of God; and as they have not committed any sin and are not soiled with the impurities of the world of nature, they are the centers of the manifestation of bounty, and the Eye of Compassion will be turned upon them.

…although the loss of a son is indeed heart-breaking and beyond the limits of human endurance, yet one who knoweth and understandeth is assured that the son hath not been lost but, rather, hath stepped from this world into another, and she will find him in the divine realm…

That beloved child addresseth thee from the hidden world: "O thou kind Mother, thank divine Providence that I have been freed from a small and gloomy cage and, like the birds of the meadows, have soared to the divine world – a world which is spacious, illumined, and ever gay and jubilant.... I have shaken off the mortal form and have raised my banner in this spiritual world. Following this separation is everlasting companionship. Thou shalt find me in the heaven of the Lord, immersed in an ocean of light."

*'Abdu'l-Bahá*

Be not sorrowful on account of the departure of thy good son. He hath indeed departed from this narrow and gloomy world which is darkened by unlimited sorrow, unto the Kingdom which is spacious, illumined, joyous and beautiful. God delivered him from this dark well and promoted him unto the Supreme Height! He gave him wings whereby he soared to the heaven of happiness. Verily this is the great mercy from Him who is precious and forgiving.

*'Abdu'l-Bahá*

O Lord, glorify his station, shelter him under the pavilion of Thy supreme mercy, cause him to enter Thy glorious paradise, and perpetuate his existence in Thine exalted rose garden, that he may plunge into the sea of light in the world of mysteries.

*'Abdu'l-Bahá*

Certain fruits, indeed, attain their fullest development only after being severed from the tree.

*Bahá'u'lláh*

It is as if a kind gardener transferreth a fresh and tender shrub from a confined place to a wide open area. This transfer is not the cause of the withering of that shrub; nay, on the contrary, it maketh it to grow and thrive, aquire freshness and delicacy, become green and bear fruit.

*'Abdu'l-Bahá*

O my God! O Thou forgiver of sins, bestower of gifts, dispeller of afflictions! Verily, I beseech Thee to forgive the sins of such as have abandoned the physical garment and have ascended to the spiritual world.

O my Lord! Purify them from trespasses, dispel their sorrows, and change their darkness into light. Cause them to enter the garden of happiness, cleanse them with the most pure water, and grant them to behold Thy splendours on the loftiest mount.

*'Abdu'l-Bahá*

Know, then, that the Lord God possesseth invisible realms which the human intellect can never hope to fathom nor the mind of man conceive. When once thou hast cleansed the channel of the spiritual sense from the pollution of this worldly life, then wilt thou breathe in the sweet scents of holiness that blow from the blissful bowers of that heavenly land.

*'Abdu'l-Bahá*

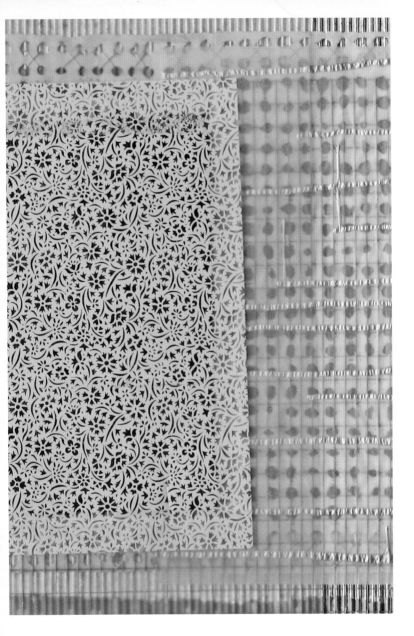

Make thou an effort, that haply in this dustheap of the mortal world thou mayest catch a fragrance from the everlasting garden, and live forever in the shadow of the peoples of this city. And when thou hast attained this highest station and come to this mightiest plane, then shalt thou gaze on the Beloved, and forget all else.

*Bahá'u'lláh*

O My servants! Sorrow not if, in these days and on this earthly plane, things contrary to your wishes have been ordained and manifested by God, for days of blissful joy, of heavenly delight, are assuredly in store for you. Worlds, holy and spiritually glorious, will be unveiled to your eyes. You are destined by Him, in this world and hereafter, to partake of their benefits, to share in their joys, and to obtain a portion of their sustaining grace. To each and every one of them you will, no doubt, attain.

*Bahá'u'lláh*

# REFERENCES

3. 'Abdu'l-Bahá, Compilations:Baha'i Scriptures, No.798 p.439

5. 'Abdu'l-Bahá, *Some Answered Questions*, (Wilmette: Bahá'i Publishing Trust, 1995), p.212

7. Bahá'u'lláh, *The Hidden Words*. Nos. 38 and 39 from the Persian.

9. Baha'u'llah. *Gleanings*, (Wilmette Publishing Trust, 1952) CLIII, p.327

11. Bahá'u'lláh, *The Hidden Words*. No.19 from the Persian.

13. 'Abdu'l-Bahá, *Selections*, (Baha'i World Centre 1982) p.241

15. Bahá'u'lláh, *Gleanings*, pp.156-57 / Bahá'u'lláh, *Tablet of visitation, Baha'i Prayers*, p.232

17. 'Abdu'l-Bahá, *Baha'i World Faith*, (US Baha'i Publishing Trust, 1976 ed) pp.254-255

19. Baha'u'llah. *Gleanings*, p.321

21. Bahá'u'lláh. *Tablet of Ahmad, Baha'i Prayers*, (Baha'i Publishing Trust, Wilmette, Illinois, 1982) p.209

23. Bahá'u'lláh, *Tablets* (Baha'i Publishing Trust, Wilmette, Illinois,1988 ) p.169

25. 'Abdu'l-Bahá, *Baha'i prayers*, p.188

27. 'Abdu'l-Bahá, *Selections*, p.171

29. Bahá'u'lláh, *The Hidden Words*. No.41 from the Persian. / 'Abdu'l-Bahá, *Selections*, p.204

31. Bahá'u'lláh, *The Hidden Words*. No. 63 from the Arabic. / No. 4 from the Persian.

33. Bahá'u'lláh, *The Seven Valleys and the Four Valleys*. (Wilmette Publishing Trust, 1991) p.4

35. 'Abdu'l-Bahá, *Some Answered Questions*, (Baha'i Publishing Trust, Wilmette, Illinois, 1984) p.241

37. Bahá'u'lláh. *Gleanings*. XXIX pp.70-71

39. Bahá'u'lláh, *The Seven Valleys and The Four Valleys*, (Qur'an 83:28) p.22.

41. Bahá'u'lláh, *Baha'i Prayers*, (Baha'i Publishing Trust, Illinois 2002) p. iii.

43. 'Abdu'l-Bahá, *Baha'i Prayers*, p.152

45. Abdu'l-Bahá, *Baha'i Prayers*, p.71

46 -47. Abdu'l-Bahá, *Divine art of living*. (Baha'i Publishing Trust, Wilmette) Pp.18-20

49. 'Abdu'l-Bahá, *Some Answered Questions*, p.225

51. Bahá'u'lláh. *Gleanings*, p.285

53. Bahá'u'lláh. *Gleanings*, p.285

54. Bahá'u'lláh, *Tablets*, p.38

57. Bahá'u'lláh, *The Hidden Words*. No.44 from the Persian.

59. Bahá'u'lláh, *The Hidden Words*. Nos. 11 and 12 from the Persian.

61. Bahá'u'lláh, *The Seven Valleys and the Four Valleys*. p.36

63. 'Abdu'l-Bahá, *Selections*. p.76

65. 'Abdu'l-Bahá, *Selections*, p.27 / Bahá'u'lláh. *Gleanings*,

LXXXI p.155-56

67. Bahá'u'lláh. *Gleanings*, LXXXI p.156

69. Bahá'u'lláh. *Gleanings*, LXXXI pp.156-157

71. Bahá'u'lláh. *Gleanings*, p.141

73. 'Abdu'l-Bahá, *Selections*, p.204, / Bahá'u'lláh.
    *Gleanings*, p.328-29

74. Bahá'u'lláh. *Gleanings*, pp.152-153 LXXIX

75. Bahá'u'lláh, *The Seven Valleys and The Four Valleys*, p.34

77. 'Abdu'l-Bahá, *Tablets of Abdul-Baha Abbas*, (New York:
    Baha'i Publishing Committee, 1930), vol.1, p.205

79. 'Abdu'l-Bahá, *The sheltering branch*, p.90

81. 'Abdu'l-Bahá, *Paris Talks*. p.90-91 / Bahá'u'lláh.
    *Gleanings*, p.161

83. 'Abdu'l-Bahá, *Paris Talks* (Bahá'i Publishing Trust
    1979) p.89 / 'Abdu'l-Bahá, *Paris Talks*, p.66

85. Bahá'u'lláh. *Gleanings*, p.159

87. Bahá'u'lláh. *Gleanings*, p.149 / adapted
    fromBahá'u'lláh. *Gleanings* XXVII

89. 'Abdu'l-Bahá, *Some Answered Questions* pp.235-236

91. 'Abdu'l-Bahá, *Bahá'i Revelation*, p.221/ 'Abdu'l-Bahá,
    *Selections*, p.189-190

93. Bahá'u'lláh. *Tablets*, vol 1 p.204

95. 'Abdu'l-Bahá, *Selections*, p.171 / Bahá'u'lláh, *Eternal
    life*, (Rustling Leaves publication, Jacqueline Mehrabi,
    2005) p.12